AI Amazon Wholesale & Arbitrage

Automate Sourcing, Analysis & Profit Tracking With AI Tools

By Joe Correa

Published by Live Stronger Faster

This book is for educational and informational purposes only. The author and publisher are not engaged in rendering legal, financial, or other professional advice. Readers should consult a qualified professional before making any financial decisions.

First Edition

Table of Contents

Overview

The world of Amazon wholesale and retail arbitrage has always rewarded speed, data, and precision, but never before has the advantage been as dramatic as it is today. The seller who can analyze more products, faster, with clearer insights and more accurate profit calculations becomes the seller who wins. Yet the traditional wholesaling and arbitrage workflow is painfully slow. You have to manually scrape supplier catalogs, evaluate hundreds or thousands of products, calculate true profitability across dozens of hidden variables, estimate demand, check for Amazon restrictions, estimate shipping and storage costs, and monitor constant price fluctuations. This meant that for years, success in arbitrage belonged only to those willing to grind through spreadsheets late into the night or to teams big enough to handle the workload. But everything changes the moment you bring artificial intelligence into the equation. With AI, a single seller can now outperform an entire team—automating product scanning, auto-analyzing catalogs, evaluating Keepa-style patterns, detecting profitable price gaps, and running margin calculations instantly. Book 9 in this series is designed to show you exactly how to use AI to become one of the most efficient and competitive Amazon wholesale and arbitrage sellers operating today. The Amazon landscape has become intensely competitive not because opportunity has disappeared, but because information moves too quickly for the average seller to keep up. Price wars, suppressed listings, shifting referral fees, increasing FBA costs, and frequent Buy Box rotations create a marketplace where the seller with the best information wins. The old days of scanning shelves with a basic app are over; now, the top sellers use AI-driven sourcing systems, automated deal analyzers, machine-learning tools that learn profitable patterns over time, and predictive algorithms that monitor marketplace volatility. The bottleneck is no longer access to suppliers—it's the ability to extract meaningful insights from supplier lists, Amazon data, and pricing history. Artificial intelligence removes this bottleneck completely. With the right AI setup, you can feed entire wholesale price lists into your system, get instant profitability outputs, receive alerts on undervalued items, and even automate conversations with suppliers to negotiate better deals. What once took days now takes minutes.

Wholesale sourcing, in particular, becomes almost unrecognizable once AI enters your workflow. Instead of manually reviewing PDFs, CSVs, or messy catalogs, AI can read them automatically, cross-reference every UPC, ASIN, and SKU with Amazon data, detect mismatches, and flag potential winners. Even better, it can evaluate demand patterns, check for seasonality, analyze review velocity, and detect whether a product is trending upward or downward.

The real breakthrough is predictive analysis: AI can forecast the probability that a listing will remain profitable based on historical sales rank, number of competing sellers, velocity of Buy Box rotation, and FBA versus FBM distribution. For years, sellers relied heavily on instinct and experience; now, AI gives beginners the ability to make decisions with the confidence of seasoned veterans. In this book, you will learn how to use AI for supplier research, catalog analysis, product verification, fake product detection, MAP violation alerts, and sourcing strategies that let you work smarter—not harder.

Retail arbitrage also enters a new era when paired with AI. Instead of scanning random aisles hoping to find a profitable product, AI tools can analyze local store inventory, price drops, hidden clearance items, and potential flips before you ever step foot in the store. Vision-based AI can scan shelves visually and instantly identify opportunities in real time—turning your camera into a product analysis engine. Meanwhile, AI models trained on millions of product patterns can detect which categories are experiencing price gaps between retail stores and Amazon, helping you target the highest-yield locations before your competitors do. For online arbitrage, AI automatically monitors retailer websites, price-match opportunities, stackable coupon deals, and limited-time offers that most sellers miss. With the right system, you receive alerts the moment a price drops enough to produce a profitable spread. Arbitrage becomes less of a hunt and more of a predictable process powered by machine intelligence.

Another game-changer AI brings to both wholesale and arbitrage is its ability to calculate true profitability—not just simple margins. Most sellers lose money not because they buy unprofitable products but because they miscalculate costs. Amazon's fee structure is complex, and mistakes add up quickly. AI solves this by automatically accounting for referral fees, FBA shipping fees, storage fees, long-term storage projections, prep costs, labeling costs, inbound shipping, carton forwarding, packaging, returns risk, and even price-war probability. Instead of guessing, you get exact numbers every time. Profitability AI systems can even analyze a product's entire price history to determine the risk of the listing tanking after you purchase inventory. This level of insight was once available only to the most advanced sellers, but AI now makes it accessible to anyone willing to use the tools.

But sourcing and profit calculations are only part of the story. AI transforms your Amazon Seller Central operations as well. Inventory management becomes automated—AI can predict sell-through rates, reorder points, and the ideal quantity to purchase. Missed restocks become a thing of the past. AI tools can monitor your pricing, automatically adjust based on Buy

Box trends, and help you avoid violating Amazon's pricing rules. They can flag potential listing problems, suppressed ASINs, hazmat reviews, and compliance issues before they impact your account. AI can even manage your communication with suppliers, generating negotiation scripts, analyzing contract terms, and identifying opportunities for better pricing or exclusivity. This book will walk you through step-by-step how to set up these automations and how to turn your Amazon wholesale or arbitrage business into a streamlined, data-driven operation.

As your business grows, the complexity of tracking profits across dozens or hundreds of SKUs increases dramatically. AI solves this too by automating profit tracking, inventory value calculation, cash flow reports, and SKU-level performance monitoring. Machine-learning tools can forecast which products are trending upward, which should be liquidated, and which deserve priority in your purchasing budget. They can detect anomalies—like sudden changes in competitor behavior, unexpected price fluctuations, or unusual returns spikes—and alert you immediately. In an industry where margins are tight and competition is fierce, these alerts can mean the difference between a profitable season and a costly mistake.

Book 9 is your blueprint for mastering this new world. Whether you're a beginner exploring your first arbitrage flips or an advanced seller sourcing pallets of wholesale inventory each month, AI levels the playing field and accelerates your growth. You no longer have to rely on manual spreadsheets, slow analysis, gut instinct, or outdated tools. You can operate with the precision and efficiency of a multimillion-dollar Amazon operation using systems that run quietly in the background while you focus on strategic decisions. This book will teach you the exact tools, prompts, workflows, and automations that the most competitive Amazon sellers use today to source smarter, evaluate faster, and scale sustainably.

By the time you finish this introduction—and ultimately this entire book—you will have a complete AI-powered business model that lets you scan more products than ever before, detect more profitable deals than your competitors, eliminate unnecessary risk, and build a wholesale and arbitrage operation that grows consistently month after month. The opportunity has never been bigger for sellers who embrace AI. You are entering the Amazon marketplace at the perfect moment—where technology can do 80% of the heavy lifting, leaving you to focus on strategy, growth, and long-term profitability. Welcome to *AI Amazon Wholesale & Arbitrage*. You're about to learn how to run one of the smartest, fastest, and most profitable sourcing systems available today—powered entirely by artificial intelligence.

Chapter 1

The AI Advantage in Wholesale & Arbitrage: How Artificial Intelligence Transforms Amazon Sourcing, Decision-Making, and Scale

Amazon wholesale and arbitrage have always relied on information, but the speed and accuracy required to compete today demand far more than human effort alone. Understanding AI's role in sourcing is the foundational skill that transforms you from a manual seller into a systems-based operator capable of reviewing thousands of products per day. The first step is recognizing that wholesale and arbitrage are fundamentally data-driven businesses. Every product is a formula—one that includes sales rank, buy box rotation, competition levels, FBA versus FBM mix, pricing history, margin, seasonality, and risk factors. Traditionally, sellers manually analyzed each of these components using spreadsheets, Keepa graphs, or vendor lists. AI completely bypasses this by extracting insights instantly from supplier catalogs, price lists, Amazon pages, and historical data, allowing you to evaluate opportunities with unmatched speed and consistency. Mastering this shift in workflow is the goal of this chapter.

Your first objective is to reframe how you source. Instead of manually opening each ASIN, scrolling through data, running calculations, and cross-checking fees, AI lets you process entire catalogs at once. The instructional foundation begins by teaching you how to feed AI structured information—such as CSV files from wholesalers—or unstructured information—such as PDFs, screenshots, or product pages. AI uses pattern recognition to interpret the data, compare product identifiers, detect mismatches, and generate profitability outputs. In doing so, it quickly eliminates products that fail basic criteria like low sales velocity, suppressed listings, oversized FBA fees, or saturated seller competition. This instantly saves hours. The goal is not to memorize product qualities but to build systems that detect those qualities automatically.

Once AI filters your product lists, you can move into deeper analysis. This involves training your AI agent on what makes a "good" or "bad" deal for your business. Thresholds such as minimum ROI, desired profit margin, sales rank range, category restrictions, MAP policies, hazmat flags, or FBA storage considerations can all be embedded into your prompts or AI workflows. The key is to think like a machine: clearly define rules, specify decision-making logic, and let AI enforce consistency. By doing this, your wholesale and arbitrage sourcing becomes predictable and scalable because the AI performs the repetitive evaluations that previously consumed your time. You step into the role of strategist rather than analyst.

Profitability is where AI offers some of the most transformative value. Instead of guessing or oversimplifying margin calculations, AI can run full profitability simulations for every product in your dataset. It accounts for referral fees, FBA shipment costs, dimensional weight, inbound freight, storage fees, prepping expenses, returns risk, and price-war probability. AI can compare the lowest seller's fulfillment method, determine the likelihood of obtaining the buy box, and evaluate whether a listing's price stability makes your profit sustainable. With arbitrage, AI evaluates local store prices, coupon stacking, cash-back opportunities, and estimated shipping costs. This reduces risk and allows you to make faster and more confident purchasing decisions.

Another important instructional component of this chapter is teaching you how to use AI to streamline supplier communication. Sourcing inventory is not just about evaluating data—it's about negotiating, requesting catalogs, joining distributor programs, and establishing profitable relationships. AI can write supplier outreach emails, craft negotiation scripts, analyze pricing structures, and generate persuasive proposals. It can review contracts to highlight hidden fees or unfavorable terms. It can even create follow-up schedules so you maintain consistent communication with your contacts. The ability to outsource these administrative tasks makes you more professional, more responsive, and more attractive to suppliers.

The next step is understanding how AI performs trend analysis. Amazon pricing and demand shift constantly. Sales rank can be misleading if you don't view it in context. Certain categories spike seasonally, while others collapse when larger brands restock. AI can read historical patterns from Keepa-style charts, detect anomalies, and forecast demand more accurately than a human can. It can predict whether a product is likely to remain profitable after you purchase inventory, or whether competition will increase. This protects your capital and helps you avoid inventory you might regret. For arbitrage, AI can track local price fluctuations, analyze regional clearance trends, predict markdown cycles, and alert you to hidden opportunities.

Finally, this chapter teaches you how to build your first AI sourcing pipeline. A sourcing pipeline is a flow: supplier list → AI analysis → filtered results → profitability evaluation → human review → purchasing decisions. The pipeline allows you to evaluate hundreds or thousands of products at scale with minimal effort. You will learn the exact prompts, workflows, and system instructions that professional Amazon sellers use today. With AI handling the heavy lifting, your sourcing time drops dramatically, and your pipeline becomes an engine that continues producing profitable leads daily.

This instructional chapter sets the foundation for everything else in the book. By the end of it, you will understand how AI interprets product data, how it evaluates opportunity, how it reduces risk, and how it creates a steady flow of profitable inventory. Whether you source wholesale pallets or clearance aisles, the principles remain the same. The power of AI is not in replacing your judgment—it's in multiplying it. You will learn to build a sourcing machine that works tirelessly and accurately, giving you the competitive advantage you need in the modern Amazon marketplace.

"The Amazon War Room"

The rain had barely stopped when Daniel stepped into his small home office, the place he jokingly called his "Amazon war room." The walls were lined with shelves filled with shipping labels, FBA prep supplies, old scanner guns, and boxes of inventory waiting to be shipped. For years he had been grinding through arbitrage—driving from Walmart to Target to Home Depot, scanning everything on clearance, searching for that one item that could turn a slow month into a profitable one. Some months he felt like he was winning. Other months, he wondered if he should quit altogether. But something new had entered the marketplace—a shift he couldn't ignore. Sellers everywhere were whispering about AI tools that could scan entire supplier catalogs, interpret pricing history, and analyze profitability thousands of times faster than a human. Daniel wasn't sure if he believed it, but after one too many late nights staring at spreadsheets, he knew he had to try something different.

His first real exposure to AI sourcing happened by accident. He received a new wholesale catalog—200 pages, cluttered with blurry images, messy descriptions, and prices that didn't match the SKUs. Normally, he would spend hours manually entering UPCs, searching for matching ASINs, clicking through Keepa graphs, and eliminating products one by one. This time, out of curiosity and mild desperation, he dragged the PDF into his AI tool. Within seconds, the system identified product matches, detected mismatches, flagged potential hazmat issues, calculated shipping estimates, and highlighted 14 items that looked profitable. Daniel stared at the screen, stunned. What would have taken him an entire weekend took less than a minute. For the first time in months, he felt something click—the sense that he wasn't just surviving arbitrage anymore. He was evolving.

Over the weeks that followed, Daniel built a new routine around his AI-powered workflow. Instead of spending mornings driving from store to store, he spent the first hour feeding supplier lists into the system. AI cross-referenced every product with Amazon's catalog, analyzing price history, demand, and competition. It didn't get tired, didn't miss details, and didn't skip products out of boredom. It reviewed every item with the same calm precision. Daniel found himself discovering deals he had never noticed before—items buried deep in catalogs that manual sellers skipped because they required too much effort to analyze. For the first time, he felt like he was competing on equal footing with larger teams.

Soon, he began using AI for more than sourcing. When a supplier sent him a wholesale contract filled with complicated terms, he uploaded it to the system. AI highlighted hidden fees, unfavorable clauses, and points of negotiation. When he wanted to request better pricing, the AI wrote messages that sounded more confident and professional than anything he had drafted before. To his surprise, suppliers responded more positively. Some even offered him access to private catalogs he had never seen. It was as if AI had quietly upgraded his identity from small seller to serious business operator.

One moment stood out more than the rest. Daniel discovered a product with an unusually stable price history and high demand—but dozens of sellers seemed to be ignoring it. His AI pointed out the reason: the supplier catalog listed the product incorrectly, causing most sellers to match it with the wrong ASIN. The actual match was profitable and had only four FBA sellers. Daniel ordered a test batch. It sold out in 72 hours. He reordered immediately, scaling the product into one of his best-performing SKUs. It felt like uncovering buried treasure—except now he had a metal detector capable of scanning the entire beach.

As the weeks turned to months, Daniel's business transformed. His sourcing pipeline became predictable, almost automatic. AI would review thousands of products, filter out the weak ones, and present a short list of promising leads. Daniel would manually verify the final few, place orders, and focus on higher-level decisions instead of drowning in spreadsheets. His stress dropped. His margins increased. And for the first time since starting his Amazon journey, he had time—time to think, plan, and grow rather than just survive.

One evening, as Daniel sat in his office reviewing another batch of AI-analyzed leads, he realized something important. AI hadn't turned him into a different person. It had simply unlocked the version of himself he always wanted to be—the version who worked smart, not endlessly; who strategized rather than reacted; who ran a business rather than a chaotic hustle. The old way of sourcing now felt prehistoric. And as he looked at the bright blue glow of his AI dashboard, he realized that he wasn't just part of the new Amazon marketplace. He was ahead of it. Chapter 1 was complete—not just in his book, but in his life. The shift had begun.

Chapter 2

AI-Powered Product & Catalog Analysis: Automating Opportunity Discovery Across Supplier Lists and Retail Sources

One of the most important skills you will ever develop in Amazon wholesale and arbitrage is the ability to create a sourcing system that runs with machine-like consistency. While Chapter 1 introduced you to the transformative power of AI for analyzing catalogs, Chapter 2 focuses on creating the structure behind your operations—your sourcing criteria, your decision-making framework, and your profit qualification rules. These elements convert AI from a helpful tool into a disciplined partner that evaluates every product using the same standards every time. Consistency is what separates profitable sellers from frustrated ones. AI gives you the ability to encode consistency into your business by defining precise rules that guide sourcing at scale.

The first instructional component of this chapter is establishing your sourcing criteria. These criteria act as your filters, protecting your capital and preventing bad buys. Too many sellers treat sourcing as an emotional process: they choose products because they "feel" good, because they like the brand, or because they see other sellers listing it. AI eliminates emotional bias by forcing you to articulate the rules behind your buying decisions. You might decide on a minimum 30% ROI, a minimum $4 net profit, a maximum 75,000 sales rank in most categories, or a maximum of five competing FBA sellers. You can also specify whether you avoid fragile products, oversized items, hazmat, gated brands, or listings with inconsistent price history. The more detailed your criteria, the more accurately AI can evaluate catalog items without your involvement.

Once your sourcing criteria are defined, the second step is teaching AI how to enforce them. This involves writing sourcing prompts that outline exactly which metrics the AI must evaluate and how it should categorize each product. You want AI to break down every potential product the same way: current price, Amazon price, buy box rotation, historical average price, competition analysis, FBA fees, ROI, margins, risk indicators, and inventory turnover. You should also embed deal-breaker rules such as "reject any ASIN with suppressed buy box," "reject if Amazon is the seller more than 60% of the time," or "reject products with declining price trends." Once you write this structure, the AI becomes your first line of defense against unprofitable inventory.

The next important instructional layer is building a consistent profitability calculator within AI. A true Amazon profit analysis goes far beyond simple ROI. It must account for Amazon referral fees, FBA pick-and-pack, dimensional weight, storage fees, inbound shipping, labeling, prep costs, poly-bag requirements, carton forwarding charges, and returns probability. AI can perform these calculations instantly, but only if you teach it which numbers to use and how to structure the analysis. For arbitrage sourcing, the calculator must also consider sales tax, coupon stacking, shipping to prep centers, and retail price variability. Your goal is to create an "AI profitability brain" that evaluates every SKU the same way—no shortcuts, no forgotten fees, no emotional buying. Over time, this dramatically increases accuracy.

Another key part of Chapter 2 is risk assessment. Profitability does not matter unless the product actually sells. AI helps you analyze price stability, competition velocity, historical demand, and category volatility. You will learn how to feed AI Keepa-style charts and ask it to evaluate long-term patterns. AI can detect decreasing price trends, seasonal spikes, brand dominance, small-seller turnover, and volatility patterns that humans often overlook. You can train AI to recognize warning signs such as repeated price crashes, frequent stockouts followed by price tanking, or listings where Amazon jumps in and out of the buy box unpredictably. Teaching AI to evaluate risk gives you long-term protection—one of the most valuable advantages in wholesale and arbitrage.

The next step involves building a sourcing pipeline that uses AI to pre-sort products into categories such as "immediate buy," "watchlist," "test buy," and "reject." This allows AI to do 80% of the work before you review anything. Once set up, the pipeline becomes a continuous loop—new supplier catalog arrives, AI analyzes it, products get categorized, and you review the top 2–5% of candidates. This removes the bottleneck of manual analysis and gives you the operational flow of a large business even if you're a solo seller. The key lesson is that AI should never replace your decision-making. It should prepare the information in a way that makes your decisions easy, fast, and consistent.

Another important instructional component is integrating AI into your daily sourcing routine. Instead of approaching sourcing randomly, you should create a structured workflow—an AI-assisted ritual—for evaluating leads. You might start each day by uploading new lists, reviewing hot leads generated overnight, checking replenishable items flagged by AI, and monitoring competitor behavior on your top SKUs. You can automate alerts so AI notifies you when a product meets your criteria, when a price drops, or when a high-performing item becomes available again. This structured routine removes the chaos from sourcing and turns your business into a predictable machine. The final instructional takeaway of Chapter 2 is learning to trust the system you've built. Many sellers sabotage themselves by constantly second-guessing their criteria, bending rules for "good" products, or buying inventory based on feelings instead of metrics. AI is only as consistent as the rules you enforce. Once your system is built, your job changes from searching for deals to managing and improving the system. This chapter teaches you how to refine criteria, improve prompts, analyze your purchasing results, and update your AI logic as you grow. Over time, your sourcing system evolves into an unstoppable engine—one that finds more leads, lowers risk, increases margins, and gives you complete control over your inventory strategy.

Daniel Didn't Feel Stressed Anymore

Daniel sat at his desk early on a Monday morning, the sun barely rising behind the blinds. His coffee was still too hot to drink, and his inbox was overflowing with supplier catalogs. In the past, this would have filled him with dread. Catalogs meant long nights, tedious searches, and endless checking of fees and rankings. But this time, things felt different. After his breakthrough with AI in Chapter 1 of his journey, he began to sense that he was building something bigger than just a better workflow. He was creating a system—a system that could finally give him the consistency and clarity he had always lacked.

He opened the first catalog of the day, a distributor he had been trying to crack for over a year. Their listings were always messy, their SKUs inconsistent, and their prices unpredictable. The old Daniel would have spent hours manually checking each item, hoping to find at least one or two winners. But the new Daniel simply dragged the PDF into the AI tool and watched the blue loading bar fill across the screen. Within moments, the AI broke down the products into ranked groups—likely winners, possible test buys, items to monitor, and automatic rejects. Daniel stared at the results, smiling. What used to take him hours now took seconds. But more importantly, everything the AI recommended made sense. It followed rules—his rules.

As he reviewed the list, he realized something he had never fully appreciated before. His business had always been unstable because his decisions were unstable. One day he would buy toys because they "felt good." The next day he would avoid them because of one bad experience. Sometimes he followed his criteria. Sometimes he ignored them entirely. The lack of consistency had cost him thousands of dollars over the years. AI was now forcing him to be disciplined. It evaluated every product using the same standards, every time. It didn't get tempted by excitement or distracted by fear. It wasn't impressed by brand names or discouraged by a category he disliked. It followed the rules he gave it. And for the first time, Daniel realized he could finally become consistent because his system was consistent. Later that afternoon, he tested a small experiment. He fed the AI two products he had previously purchased manually—one good buy and one bad buy. For the profitable product, the AI instantly highlighted strong price stability, low competition, and a margin profile consistent with his criteria. For the losing product, the AI flagged three warning signs he had missed: a long-term downward price trend, heavy Amazon involvement, and poor historical ROI. Seeing the AI's breakdown almost made him laugh. The system wasn't just analyzing products—it was teaching him how to think more clearly. It was showing him what he should have seen years ago.

That night, Daniel reflected on how far he had come. He remembered the stress he used to feel every time he made a sourcing decision. The uncertainty. The fear of losing money. The frustration of guessing. Now he could see the difference. Before, he was acting like a gambler—hoping for good outcomes. Now he was acting like a strategist—engineering good outcomes. AI didn't just speed up his sourcing. It rewired his decision-making. It gave him confidence that came from structure, not luck.

A few days later, he experienced his first real test. A supplier emailed him a “special buy” list filled with products marked as limited stock. These lists always created pressure—sellers felt they had to rush or miss out. Daniel uploaded the list into his AI system, expecting a few decent opportunities. But surprisingly, the AI rejected almost all the items. The margins were poor, the competition was heavy, and several listings showed steep downward trends. In the past, Daniel would have bought at least three or four items anyway, convincing himself that demand would spike or that other sellers were wrong. But this time, he didn’t argue. He followed the system.

Three days later, he checked the listings out of curiosity. Nearly every one of them had already begun to tank—competition increasing, prices dropping, Buy Box rotating unpredictably. If he had acted emotionally, he would have tied up hundreds of dollars in bad inventory. Instead, he watched from the sidelines as other sellers made the mistakes he used to make. He felt proud—not because he avoided a bad buy, but because he was finally operating with discipline.

One evening, as Daniel reviewed another batch of leads generated by AI, he realized something powerful. He didn’t feel stressed anymore. He didn't feel lost or overwhelmed. He didn't feel like he was rolling the dice every time he purchased inventory. For the first time since he started selling on Amazon, he felt in control. Not because he magically became smarter, but because he built a system that made smart decisions for him.

He leaned back in his chair, watching the AI generate another perfect breakdown of a new supplier list. He smiled and took a sip of his now-cold coffee. The journey had changed. He wasn't chasing deals anymore. He was running a system. And that system was working.

Chapter 3

Intelligent Deal Validation & Risk Filtering: Using AI to Eliminate Bad Buys Before They Cost You Money

One of the most powerful ways to elevate your Amazon wholesale and arbitrage business is by learning how to use AI for catalog analysis at scale. In earlier chapters, you learned the importance of consistent sourcing criteria and the value of AI in replacing slow, manual evaluation methods. In Chapter 3, you go deeper into building AI systems that can process entire supplier catalogs, bulk price lists, PDF product sheets, retail store inventory data, and online clearance listings in minutes. The goal is not only speed, but pattern recognition—training your AI to evaluate products not in isolation, but in the context of marketplaces, competition, volatility, and historical performance. This turns your sourcing process into a scalable machine capable of reviewing thousands of ASINs with accuracy that surpasses human capability.

The instructional core of this chapter begins by showing you how to train AI to interpret different types of supplier inputs. Supplier information rarely comes clean. Some wholesalers send CSV files with clear UPC fields and pricing; others send blurry PDFs, inconsistent SKUs, outdated images, non-standard product names, or incomplete fields. AI can interpret all of these formats. When trained properly, AI can extract product names, UPCs, ASINs, brand data, packaging information, MSRP, wholesale cost, case quantity, MAP policies, and even shipping information from any document format. The key is teaching the AI to normalize messy data—converting it into structured fields that can be analyzed quickly and accurately. This replaces hours of manual cleaning and removes the frustration that stops many sellers from exploring new suppliers.

Once AI has interpreted the catalog, the next step is matching supplier products to Amazon listings. Traditionally, this process took enormous time because sellers had to manually search Amazon by UPC or title, compare listings, verify images, check variations, and exclude mismatches. AI can do this instantly at scale. It cross-references supplier products with Amazon data and identifies the most likely ASIN matches. It detects mismatches by evaluating image similarity, title keywords, brand consistency, and variation attributes. It can even determine whether the supplier product belongs to a parent listing, a variant, or an entirely incorrect ASIN. With proper prompts, AI can assign confidence levels to each match, allowing you to quickly identify strong opportunities without getting bogged down by errors.

Another instructional focus is training AI to analyze product history and pricing behavior. AI can evaluate historical price charts, sales rank trends, review velocity, number of competing sellers, buy box stability, and average profit windows. It can identify whether a product has stable, predictable margins or whether it suffers from price tanking, excess competition, or temporary artificial price spikes. AI can also evaluate how Amazon behaves on the listing—whether Amazon frequently controls the buy box, goes out of stock often, or competes aggressively with third-party sellers. These insights prevent costly mistakes by highlighting products that may appear profitable in a snapshot but pose long-term risk.

The chapter also focuses on batch profitability analysis. For wholesale and arbitrage sellers, evaluating products one at a time is inefficient. AI allows you to run batch profitability analysis for entire supplier lists, evaluating each SKU's total cost structure, Amazon fee breakdown, ROI, margin, and estimated units sold per month. It can detect whether a product has enough demand for your buying quantity, whether the profit remains stable at different price levels, and whether competition will eat into your margins. You can train AI to compute profitability under multiple scenarios—current buy box, 30-day average, 90-day average, seasonal fluctuations, and anticipated competition levels. This gives you a holistic view of a product's earning potential rather than a single moment-in-time calculation.

Another important part of this chapter is teaching AI to categorize products into sourcing actions. Instead of overwhelming you with raw data, you want your AI to automatically assign each product to categories such as: strong buy, test buy, replenish, seasonal opportunity, restricted but promising, mismatch, avoid due to Amazon presence, or reject due to poor profit metrics. This saves you hours and ensures that your decision-making remains consistent. Over time, your AI becomes capable of identifying patterns in your best purchases, learning the traits of products that succeed in your business, and improving its recommendations accordingly.

You also learn how to use AI to analyze variations. Variation listings on Amazon can be profitable or dangerous depending on how traffic and reviews are distributed among children. AI can break down which variant receives the most sales, which has the most reviews, which price point sells best, and whether your supplier's product aligns with the dominant variant. This prevents major mistakes like purchasing a slow-moving variation simply because it appears on a popular listing.

The final instructional element in this chapter is building an AI catalog pipeline that triggers automated alerts. When supplier catalogs update, when prices drop, when Amazon restocks, when a competitor exits a listing, or when seasonal demand increases, your AI can notify you immediately. These alerts give you real-time advantage—allowing you to enter listings at optimal moments or secure inventory before other sellers discover the opportunity. Over time, your AI becomes a sourcing assistant that runs 24/7, watching the market even when you're sleeping, and presenting opportunities that were invisible to manual sellers.

He Had Built Something

Daniel sat on the edge of his chair, staring at the giant wholesale catalog that had just landed in his inbox—a massive 300-item seasonal catalog from a supplier he had been trying to work with for months. In the past, receiving a catalog like this made him feel overwhelmed. He remembered nights where he stayed up until 2 a.m., cross-referencing UPCs, copying ASINs into spreadsheets, and trying to make sense of scattered data. Back then, he felt like every catalog was a mountain he wasn't sure he could climb. But now, things were different. He had built something—an AI system that changed the way he worked forever. And today, he was about to put it to the test with the largest catalog he had ever processed.

He dragged the PDF into the AI tool and watched the screen pulse with activity. The AI didn't just read the catalog—it decoded it. It interpreted every messy line of text, extracted UPCs from blurry images, organized variations into structured data, and matched products to ASINs with stunning accuracy. Daniel watched the results populate in real time. Thousands of lines of analysis spilled across his screen—buy box rotations, historical averages, FBA fees, ROI estimates, sales rank patterns, and risk indicators. It was like having a team of analysts working at superhuman speed.

As he scrolled through the output, Daniel noticed something unusual. One of the products—a small kitchen appliance—was flagged by the AI as highly profitable, despite looking unremarkable at first glance. The listing showed stable pricing, low competition, strong demand, and seasonal lift predicted for the upcoming months. But what caught Daniel's attention was the AI's note: "Hidden variation opportunity." The AI noticed that the supplier's product matched the bestselling child variation, not the slower variants. Daniel realized that without AI, he would have never caught this nuance. Most sellers would match the listing without noticing that only one variation accounted for 80% of total sales. This was a perfect example of what the AI could see that humans often couldn't.

A moment later, the AI flagged a product that Daniel had sourced the previous year and lost money on. He clicked the breakdown and saw a detailed explanation of why the product still posed danger: Amazon frequently jumped on and off the listing, price history showed instability, and new sellers entered the listing almost weekly. Daniel smiled. The AI wasn't just protecting his wallet—it was teaching him. It was reminding him of patterns he used to miss, patterns that had cost him hundreds of dollars.

That afternoon, he decided to test something new. He uploaded an online retailer clearance page into the system—no UPCs, no clean data, just messy HTML and product descriptions. Within seconds, the AI parsed each item, extracted information, matched listings, and ranked opportunities. Daniel watched as it highlighted a small electronics accessory with a massive price gap between the clearance price and the Amazon price. The AI predicted strong sales velocity and stable margins. He checked the listing manually to verify, and everything matched. It felt like magic—like the AI was showing him hidden doorways in stores he had shopped in for years.

Over the next few days, Daniel built a rhythm. He uploaded catalogs in the morning, reviewed AI-sorted opportunities at lunch, and placed orders in the afternoon. It no longer took emotional energy to source. There was no guessing, no stress, no second-guessing himself. The AI handled the chaos. It turned messy catalogs into clean data. It turned confusion into clarity. And as he watched his sourcing confidence grow, he realized something profound: this wasn't just automation. This was transformation.

But the moment that truly changed everything happened late one night. Daniel received a sudden price drop alert from his AI system. It detected that a high-demand retail item had gone on clearance at a regional store near him. The AI predicted that the price gap created a narrow but extremely profitable window before other sellers caught on. Without hesitating, Daniel jumped into his car and drove to the store. When he arrived, he found exactly three units left—the exact quantity the AI predicted based on store inventory patterns. He bought all three, listed them, and they sold within hours at the full price. It wasn't the profit that moved him. It was the accuracy. For the first time in his career, he felt like he wasn't reacting to the market—he was ahead of it.

As Daniel sat back in his office later that night, reviewing the day's wins, he felt something shift inside him. He wasn't just becoming a better seller. He was becoming the architect of a system that could scale endlessly, a system that made him sharper, faster, smarter, and more confident than ever before.

The chaos of arbitrage was fading. The clarity of automation was taking its place. And Daniel knew, deep down, that he was only getting started.

Chapter 4

AI Risk Assessment & Listing Stability Analysis: Detecting Price Volatility, Competition Traps, and Amazon Interference

One of the most critical components of becoming a highly profitable Amazon wholesale and arbitrage seller is mastering AI-powered risk assessment. While sourcing criteria and catalog automation help you identify potential opportunities at scale, risk assessment ensures that you only act on opportunities with the highest probability of producing consistent, sustainable profit. In Chapter 4, you learn how to teach AI to examine risk factors across price, competition, listing structure, historical volatility, category behavior, and Amazon involvement. The goal is to elevate your sourcing beyond simple margin checks and transform your evaluation process into one that resembles institutional investing rather than speculative buying. When you learn how to get AI to think in terms of risk versus reward, your buying decisions become significantly smarter and your losses decrease dramatically.

The instructional foundation of this chapter begins with understanding that risk on Amazon comes in many forms. Some risks are obvious—such as Amazon controlling the buy box or a low sales rank masking a sudden crash in price history—but many risks are subtle and impossible to detect manually at scale. AI allows you to analyze signals that normally require years of experience to interpret correctly. These signals include rapid seller turnover, unstable buy box rotation, suppressed listings, inconsistent fulfillment methods, abnormal review patterns, variation cannibalization, and historical pricing anomalies. You will learn how to build AI prompts that look beyond the surface and evaluate the deeper structure of each listing. This allows you to avoid products that appear profitable in the moment but are actually collapsing beneath the surface.

The next instructional component teaches you how to use AI to evaluate competition volatility. Competition is one of the most underestimated risk factors in wholesale and arbitrage. Even a product with great margins can fail if seller count increases rapidly or if an aggressive competitor lowers prices below sustainable levels. AI can track competitor behavior by analyzing how often sellers enter and exit the listing, how frequently prices change, and whether the buy box rotates or remains fixed. It can identify patterns such as new sellers tanking prices, experienced sellers dominating the listing, or seasonal sellers entering temporarily. Training AI to detect competition volatility gives you a more realistic view of future profitability and helps you avoid buying into listings where success depends on unpredictable behavior from other sellers.

Another key instructional focus is price history volatility. AI does not simply look at current price—it analyzes historical pricing patterns to determine whether the listing is stable, trending upward, or collapsing. You will learn how to train AI to interpret Keepa-style data such as 30-day average price, 90-day average price, buy box variance, Amazon stock alerts, and sudden price compression. AI can detect whether the listing's price is being held artificially high due to temporary stockouts or whether a recent drop indicates the beginning of a long-term decline. By evaluating pricing behavior over time rather than a single snapshot, AI helps you avoid one of the most common and costly mistakes in sourcing: buying into a listing right before the price collapses.

In addition to historical analysis, AI can perform forward-looking risk projections. Using sales velocity, seasonality data, competitor behavior, and pricing cycles, AI can forecast the likelihood that a product will remain profitable for the next 30–90 days. This forward-thinking approach allows you to time your purchases strategically, entering listings at moments when margins are strongest and competition is lowest. You will learn how to create prompts that ask AI to project future conditions rather than simply evaluate present ones. This transforms your sourcing from reactive to predictive and gives you an edge over sellers who only analyze static data.

Another instructional element of this chapter involves listing stability. AI can identify indicators of a weak or unstable listing, such as mismatched variations, inconsistent product categorization, keyword suppression, incorrect parent-child relationships, or sudden changes in the buy box algorithm. These structural issues can lead to suppressed listings, lost ranking, or reduced visibility—problems that often catch inexperienced sellers off guard. Teaching AI to evaluate listing integrity allows you to avoid products at risk of being delisted or suppressed shortly after purchase. You will gain a system that examines a listing holistically rather than just focusing on immediate profitability.

The chapter also teaches you how AI evaluates brand-level risk. Some brands are known for issuing IP complaints, enforcing strict MAP policies, or aggressively monitoring unauthorized sellers. AI can analyze brand behavior by searching for patterns of complaints, marketplace conditions, legal language, seller discussions, and historical enforcement. You will learn how to prompt AI to flag brands with high complaint risk or inconsistent enforcement patterns. This prevents account health issues and protects your long-term ability to sell.

The final instructional component in this chapter is combining all risk factors—pricing, competition, Amazon behavior, structural stability, brand risk, and seasonality—into a single AI risk profile. This risk profile becomes your sourcing compass. Instead of manually juggling dozens of data points, you will have AI deliver a concise, reliable risk summary for every product. This summary turns complex sourcing decisions into simple action steps. Over time, you will notice that your sourcing becomes sharper, your accuracy increases, and your profitability stabilizes. By mastering AI-powered risk assessment, you elevate yourself above the average Amazon seller and enter a tier of decision-making that resembles professional trading rather than retail product buying.

The System That Protected Him

Daniel sat in his office late one evening, the glow of his monitors illuminating the room as he scrolled through yet another promising product. On the surface, everything looked perfect—high margins, great sales rank, and a stable buy box price. A year ago, he would have jumped on the opportunity immediately. Back then, if the numbers looked good, he bought. And sometimes it worked. But sometimes, it didn't.

There were products where the price tanked the moment he received them, others where Amazon came back in stock and crushed the listing, and still others where competitors flooded the listing overnight and destroyed profitability. Those painful experiences had shaped him more than he realized. He now knew what many sellers didn't: profit is only real if risk is controlled.

He uploaded the product into his AI system and waited. Within seconds, a detailed analysis appeared on the screen. The AI flagged the product with a high risk score. Daniel leaned forward, intrigued. The tool explained that although the price looked stable over the last 30 days, the 90-day chart showed repeated crashes caused by competition spikes. The seller count had fluctuated dramatically, with newcomers repeatedly entering the listing and undercutting prices. Even worse, Amazon had intermittently jumped in and out of the listing, lowering the buy box every time they appeared. Daniel felt a familiar chill. He remembered losing money on a similar pattern the previous year. Without AI, he would have missed it again. But this time, he closed the listing without hesitation. The system had protected him.

The next morning, Daniel experienced a different kind of lesson. His AI flagged a product he had dismissed at first glance—a household item with modest margins. Curious, he opened the breakdown. The AI highlighted unusually stable price history, consistent seller count, strong review velocity, and predictable sales rank. Competition was healthy but not aggressive. The listing structure was clean. Amazon stayed out of the buy box. The product wasn't flashy or exciting, but it was reliable. Stable. Predictable. Daniel realized it was exactly the kind of product he needed more of—products that didn't keep him awake at night. He ordered a test batch. It sold smoothly, exactly as the AI predicted.

That afternoon, he uploaded a massive 500-item supplier catalog into the system. As the AI analyzed each product, Daniel noticed something interesting. The AI wasn't just telling him what to buy or avoid. It was teaching him a new way of thinking—how to identify patterns, how to spot hidden dangers, how to understand the market like a strategist instead of a gambler. When the AI flagged a popular toy as risky, Daniel checked the data manually. The price had indeed been tanking every holiday season after massive restocks. He had seen this toy on Instagram and TikTok all month. It looked like a goldmine, but AI saw the truth beneath the hype. It saw what most sellers would miss until it was too late.

Later in the evening, Daniel recalled one of the hardest lessons of his early selling days. He had bought 120 units of a beauty product that showed great margins. Without warning, Amazon returned to the listing and held the buy box for months. Daniel couldn't compete. He lost almost everything. That memory had haunted him for years. But now, as he watched the AI evaluate brand risk factors and predict Amazon's stocking behavior, he felt a sense of peace. He finally had a system that could prevent disasters before they happened. He finally had something he could trust.

One night, just as he was getting ready to close his laptop, the AI sent him an alert. A seasonal product was entering a period where sales velocity historically spiked while competition typically dropped. The AI predicted a narrow window of opportunity. Daniel verified the data and agreed. He placed a carefully measured order, trusting the system. Two weeks later, every unit sold out at premium margins. It was one of the cleanest, most efficient profits he had ever made.

As Daniel sat back in his chair, he realized that risk assessment wasn't just about avoiding bad products. It was about stepping into the future with clarity. It was about building a business where profit wasn't based on luck but on intelligence. AI had given him that intelligence. It had become his silent partner, watching every detail, analyzing every risk, and guiding him toward choices that created stability and growth.

For the first time in his entrepreneurial life, Daniel no longer feared the unknown. He understood it. He anticipated it. He managed it. And he smiled, knowing that he was no longer playing the Amazon game blindly. He was playing it with vision.

Chapter 5

Building an AI Profitability Engine: Calculating True Net Profit, Fees, and Multi-Scenario Outcomes Automatically

The most profitable Amazon wholesale and arbitrage sellers are not those who simply find great products—they are the ones who build sophisticated AI-driven profitability systems that calculate true profit with precision. Chapter 5 focuses on one of the most important and often misunderstood components of your business: constructing an AI-powered profitability engine that eliminates guesswork, reduces risk, and helps you make buying decisions with a level of confidence and accuracy that manual sellers can never achieve. Every product has a story that goes far beyond cost and selling price. True profitability includes Amazon fees, inbound shipping, prep costs, labeling, fulfillment method differences, competition behavior, seasonal price fluctuations, and the probability of maintaining the buy box. This chapter teaches you how to train AI to account for all variables so you can evaluate products with the sophistication of an institutional investor analyzing financial assets.

The instructional foundation begins with understanding how to break profitability into layers. Most new sellers look at only one layer: the difference between cost and selling price. Advanced sellers look at two layers: cost, price, and fees. But professional-level sellers analyze profits across multiple dimensions, such as the correlation between buy box price and competition levels, historical pricing averages, price volatility cycles, inbound shipping costs relative to dimensional weight, and the projected probability of returns based on product category. AI is uniquely capable of processing all of these factors simultaneously. When trained correctly, it evaluates profitability across dozens of variables in seconds and provides a realistic picture of what you will actually make—not what you hope to make. This allows you to eliminate emotional buying and replace it with disciplined, data-backed decision-making.

Another major instructional focus of this chapter is teaching AI how to calculate Amazon's complex fee structure accurately. FBA pick-and-pack fees vary by size, weight, category, and storage season. Referral fees vary by category and can fluctuate during promotions or special events. Storage fees increase during Q4, and small changes in dimensional weight can significantly impact profitability. AI allows you to input custom prompts that calculate all fees precisely and automatically. You will learn how to instruct AI to build a complete breakdown that includes referral fees, FBA fees, storage fees, inbound shipping estimates, label costs, poly-bag requirements, carton forwarding, and prep center fees. By making these calculations part of your AI workflow instead of manual spreadsheets, you remove human error and gain the ability to analyze hundreds of products at once using consistent, accurate logic.

The next instructional component is training AI to perform multi-scenario forecasting. A product might be profitable at today's price, but what if the buy box drops by 5%, 10%, or 15%? What if competition increases? What if Amazon restocks? AI can simulate profitability under different market scenarios so you can assess risk and choose your buying quantities more intelligently. You will learn how to prompt AI to calculate profit under multiple price points—current buy box, 30-day average, 90-day average, and predicted price after competition shift. By evaluating products across multiple potential outcomes, you gain a deeper understanding of whether the deal is sustainable or fragile. This method dramatically reduces the chances of buying into listings that collapse shortly after you invest.

Another key instructional area is estimating inbound shipping and prep costs. Too many sellers underestimate these expenses, leading to surprising losses that were avoidable. AI can calculate average shipping costs per pound or per cubic foot, estimate prep labor costs, and determine whether a product requires special packaging that increases fees. AI can also factor in prep center geography, regional freight cost differences, and carton restrictions. This ensures that your profit estimates reflect reality rather than optimistic assumptions. Once you teach AI how to calculate these costs consistently, you will never again underestimate the impact of shipping, prep, or logistics on your margins.

In addition to cost analysis, profitability forecasting also includes analyzing expected sell-through rates. A product may have strong margins but poor velocity, causing your capital to sit in inventory for months. AI can estimate sales velocity based on historical rank, review growth patterns, seasonal fluctuations, and competitor analysis. You will learn how to create prompts that ask AI to determine how quickly a product is likely to sell through 10, 20, 50, or 100 units. This allows you to make smarter decisions about how much inventory to buy. A smaller order with fast turnover can sometimes produce more profit than a larger order that ties up your capital for too long.

Another important aspect of this chapter is helping AI detect hidden profitability traps—situations where a product looks profitable on the surface but contains deeper risks that reduce real profit. For example, AI can detect listings where the cheapest seller is FBM, where returns are unusually high, where the buy box rotates unpredictably, or where Amazon is likely to suppress the listing due to incomplete variations or incorrect category placement. You will learn how to build prompts that ask AI to search for these traps explicitly. This protects your business from avoidable losses and helps you identify products that are structurally more secure.

The final instructional takeaway of this chapter is integrating your AI profitability model into your daily sourcing pipeline. Once your system is built, AI should automatically analyze every product you consider, calculate realistic profits under multiple scenarios, and flag opportunities or risks before you make decisions. This automation gives you confidence, speed, and accuracy that manual sellers simply cannot match. As your AI continues to evaluate products over time, it learns which types of opportunities match your business model and which do not, becoming increasingly aligned with your sourcing strategy. A well-trained AI profitability engine becomes your most valuable asset—one that works tirelessly, never gets tired, never rushes, and always gives you accurate numbers.

Why Daniel Stared at the Screen

Daniel had made plenty of mistakes in his Amazon career, but the ones that hurt the most were the profitable mistakes—deals that looked amazing on the surface but quietly drained his money once all the unseen costs revealed themselves. He remembered one shipment vividly. It was a stack of oversized fitness products he purchased because the margins looked incredible. By the time he paid prep fees, inbound shipping, oversized FBA fees, and storage charges for slow-moving items, the profit evaporated. He made almost nothing, and the frustration lingered in his mind for months. Those experiences taught him that margins could lie—and that sellers who relied on simple math were gambling with incomplete information.

But now, as he sat in his office analyzing products with his new AI system, everything felt different. He uploaded a promising product from a supplier catalog—one with a strong buy box price and low competition. A year ago, he would have purchased immediately. Instead, he waited for the AI to run its profitability calculations. When the results appeared, Daniel blinked in surprise. The AI estimated FBA fees that were far higher than he expected. It flagged the product as "dangerous margin shrinkage" due to its unusual dimensions. It ran multi-scenario forecasts showing that if the buy box dropped even 10%, the product would become unprofitable. Daniel realized he had almost repeated one of his old mistakes. Without AI, he would have been blind to the real numbers. Now, he saw everything clearly.

Later that afternoon, Daniel uploaded a different product—one he almost skipped because the margins looked average. But the AI saw something he didn't. It ran a 90-day average analysis and discovered that the buy box price had remained incredibly stable for months, even during competition spikes. The AI noted that the product had a consistently low return rate, high review velocity, and predictable sales rank fluctuations. It calculated realistic profitability under multiple scenarios and revealed that the product had extremely reliable margins. Daniel felt a quiet excitement. This was the kind of product he wanted—boring, predictable, stable, consistent profit. The kind most new sellers ignore because it doesn't look flashy at first glance. He ordered 30 units, and within a week, they were selling smoothly. He felt like he had discovered a secret that only experienced sellers understand: real profitability lies in consistency, not excitement.

One evening, Daniel decided to revisit an old supplier he had stopped buying from because the margins had always been thin. Out of curiosity, he uploaded their entire price list into the AI system. When the analysis came back, Daniel stared at the screen. The AI identified several overlooked items with unique profit structures. These items appeared unprofitable under simple calculations, but when AI accounted for low inbound shipping costs, efficient prep requirements, and rapid sell-through rates, the real profits were surprisingly strong.

Daniel felt a mixture of emotions—regret that he never saw these opportunities before, and gratitude that he had a tool that could finally reveal what he had missed for years.

Then came the moment that truly changed everything. Daniel uploaded a bundle opportunity—a combination of two products from the same supplier. In the past, bundle sourcing intimidated him because calculating fees was complicated. But the AI broke everything down effortlessly. It evaluated the historical performance of similar bundles, calculated combined FBA fees, analyzed customer behavior patterns, and projected profits under multiple price points. The analysis was so thorough, so precise, that Daniel felt a wave of confidence. He placed a small test order. When the bundle sold out within days, he felt the same rush he felt years ago when he made his first profitable flip—but this time, it wasn't luck. It was strategy. It was intelligence. It was AI.

Over the next few weeks, Daniel began trusting the system more and more. Not blindly, but thoughtfully. He started asking AI to explain its reasoning, to break down every cost, to project every risk, to simulate every scenario. And the more he relied on these predictions, the more accurate his decisions became. He no longer felt anxious placing orders. He no longer feared the hidden costs that used to keep him awake at night. His business felt calm, controlled, strategic.

One night, as he looked over his profitability dashboard, Daniel realized something profound. He wasn't just becoming a better Amazon seller. He was becoming the kind of business owner he had always wanted to be—disciplined, informed, confident, and in control. His profitability engine wasn't just calculating numbers. It was calculating clarity. And for the first time, Daniel could see his path forward with absolute certainty.

Chapter 6

AI Replenishment Forecasting & Inventory Control: Scaling Replens Without Stockouts, Overbuying, or Cash Flow Stress

Chapter 6 focuses on building one of the most important systems in your Amazon wholesale and arbitrage business: AI-powered replenishment forecasting and inventory management. While many sellers obsess over sourcing new products, the most consistently profitable sellers understand that long-term success comes from managing replenishable inventory—products you can purchase repeatedly, profitably, with predictable demand and stable margins. This chapter teaches you how to use AI to identify, forecast, and manage replenishable products with a level of precision that would be impossible manually. When you build an AI-driven replenishment engine, your business gains stability, reduced workload, consistent profit, and a compounding effect that grows your revenue month after month.

The instructional foundation begins with understanding what makes a replenishable product valuable. A replen is not simply a product that sells well; it is a product with predictable sales velocity, stable margins, low volatility, and consistent supplier availability. Many sellers mistakenly confuse one-time wins with replan potential. AI solves this problem by analyzing long-term historical data instead of relying on short-term performance. You will learn how to train AI to evaluate sales rank over time, analyze buy box stability across seasons, detect patterns in seller count fluctuations, and identify products that maintain consistent profitability. This allows AI to filter out unstable products and flag true replens that can form the backbone of your business.

The next major instructional concept involves demand forecasting. AI can evaluate historical sales patterns—daily, weekly, monthly, and yearly—to determine how many units you are likely to sell in future periods. Unlike manual forecasting, which is often influenced by emotion or guesswork, AI forecasting uses statistical modeling, historical price cycles, and competition analysis to generate realistic predictions. You will learn how to prompt AI to generate 30-day, 60-day, and 90-day projections based on variables such as price stability, review velocity, listing exposure, and seasonal demand. This type of forecasting prevents two of the most dangerous mistakes in Amazon selling: running out of stock or over-ordering. By maintaining optimal inventory levels, you maximize profit while minimizing risk. Another core instructional component is identifying replenishment triggers. Triggers are automated signals that tell you when it's time to reorder inventory based on projected sales and current stock levels. AI can evaluate how many units are in Amazon's warehouses, how many are in transit, your average daily sales rate, and anticipated demand surges. You will learn how to create prompts that instruct AI to notify you when your inventory falls below defined thresholds. This turns replenishment from a reactive task into a proactive system, ensuring you never lose momentum on profitable SKUs. Over time, AI can even learn your preferred order quantities and adjust recommendations based on supplier lead times.

The chapter also teaches you how to integrate supplier availability into your replenishment model. AI can analyze supplier catalogs to detect whether a product is seasonal, permanently stocked, or frequently out of stock. It can monitor supplier price fluctuations, bulk discounts, case pack requirements, and shipment schedules. By combining supplier data with Amazon demand forecasting, AI can determine the ideal times to reorder inventory to secure the best margins and ensure consistent availability. This prevents last-minute scrambling and gives you a competitive advantage by locking in stable supply when other sellers face shortages.

Another instructional focus is cash flow forecasting. Replens create ongoing profit, but they also require disciplined cash flow management. AI can calculate how much capital is tied up in inventory, how long it takes to recover your investment, and when you can expect profitable returns. It can estimate reorder cycles and help you determine whether you have the financial capacity to scale certain SKUs. AI can also simulate the impact of increasing your order quantities, allowing you to explore growth opportunities safely. This transforms inventory management from an emotional guessing game into a strategic financial decision.

The chapter then expands into multi-SKU portfolio management. Instead of thinking about each product individually, AI helps you manage your entire replenishment catalog like a diversified investment portfolio. It can identify which SKUs provide the highest return, which should be prioritized for scale, which are at risk of becoming unprofitable, and which should be discontinued. By evaluating each product's risk profile, profitability trend, velocity pattern, and supplier stability, AI can recommend where to allocate your purchasing budget for maximum return. This elevates your business from chaotic order-taking to a structured, data-driven operation.

The final instructional component of this chapter involves automating your replenishment dashboard. AI can consolidate all SKU performance data into daily or weekly reports that highlight your inventory levels, forecasted sales, recommended order quantities, expected profitability, and any risk signals. Over time, your replenishment dashboard becomes your business control center. Instead of manually checking listings or relying on incomplete spreadsheets, you gain a real-time view of your entire operation. With this system in place, your business becomes significantly easier to manage, more predictable, and far more scalable. AI allows you to focus your energy on strategy, growth, and supplier relationships while it handles the complexity of forecasting and inventory management.

The AI-driven Replenishment Engine

Daniel sat at his desk staring at the numbers on his screen—long columns of inventory data, sell-through rates, and pending shipments. In his early days as a seller, these numbers always felt like noise. He never knew how much to order. Sometimes he bought too much and watched boxes gather dust in his garage. Other times, he sold out too quickly and missed weeks of potential profit because he didn't reorder in time. Inventory management had always been the invisible weight pressing against his success. But today, something felt different. Today, he had a new system—an AI-driven replenishment engine he had spent weeks developing. And today was the day he would use it to transform chaos into clarity.

He uploaded the latest sales data from Amazon and waited for the AI to process it. The system analyzed every SKU—its sales rank, its buy box history, its competition patterns, its price stability—and then cross-referenced that with his current inventory levels and supplier availability. Within moments, the AI displayed a detailed summary of which products needed reordering, how many units he should purchase, and when he needed to place each order to avoid running out of stock. Daniel stared at the screen in disbelief. For years, he had guessed these numbers. Now the answers were right in front of him, precise and undeniable.

His eyes fell on one particular product—a household essential he had been selling for months. It was one of his most reliable performers, but he had always underestimated how quickly it sold. The AI projected that he would sell out in 11 days and recommended placing a reorder within the next 48 hours. It even calculated the ideal quantity based on his supplier's case packs, past velocity, and expected seasonal lift. Daniel felt a rush of relief. He wouldn't have discovered this timing on his own. He would have lost the listing momentum, the ranking, and the steady profit stream that had quietly become an anchor in his business.

A few minutes later, the AI flagged a different product—a toy that had recently spiked in demand. Daniel felt a pang of excitement. A year ago, that excitement would have pushed him to place a large reorder immediately. But the AI offered a more measured perspective. It projected that the demand spike was temporary and warned that competition was rising quickly. The system recommended a small replenishment order—a test quantity—rather than a full commitment. Daniel nodded. This was the kind of discipline he always struggled with. AI wasn't just helping him make decisions; it was helping him avoid mistakes born from emotion and impatience.

Later that afternoon, Daniel reviewed the AI's portfolio analysis. It highlighted his most profitable SKUs, ranked them by stability, and suggested which products he should scale next. One replen stood out—a kitchen gadget he had nearly abandoned when its sales slowed for a few weeks. The AI analysis revealed that the slowdown was seasonal and projected that demand would rise again in the coming month. Daniel felt a wave of satisfaction. Without this system, he would have written off a consistently profitable product because of a temporary dip. Now he could reorder with confidence, knowing he wasn't making decisions in the dark.

One moment that surprised him came when the AI reviewed his cash flow projection. It calculated how much capital he had tied up in inventory and how quickly he could recover his investment if he increased order quantities on his most stable SKUs. It offered a recommendation to scale two of his best performers—gradually, safely, intelligently. Daniel leaned back in his chair, taking it all in. For the first time since he started selling on Amazon, he felt like he had a CFO working alongside him—a data-powered strategist who understood his business better than he ever had.

As evening settled in, Daniel processed his replenishment orders with a sense of calm he'd never experienced before. No second-guessing. No fear. No stress. He placed orders because the numbers made sense, not because he hoped they would. He felt a lift in his chest—a quiet confidence that had been missing for years. His business no longer felt like a roller coaster of highs and lows. It felt steady. Predictable. Intelligent.

Later that night, as he closed his laptop, Daniel realized something powerful. Replenishment wasn't just about maintaining inventory. It was about building a foundation—a stable core of reliable products that created consistent profit month after month. And AI had given him the ability to build that foundation with precision. For years, he had dreamed of creating a business that felt secure, scalable, and under control. Now, with his AI replenishment system in place, he finally had the system that could make it real. Daniel smiled, knowing that tomorrow's sales were no longer a mystery. They were a plan.

Chapter 7

AI Supplier Management & Negotiation Systems: Automating Communication, Pricing Strategy, and Relationship Building

Chapter 7 focuses on building AI-powered supplier management systems—one of the most overlooked but essential elements of scaling a profitable wholesale and arbitrage business. Most sellers believe their success depends solely on finding good products, but in reality, the strength of your supplier network determines the quality, consistency, and durability of your business over time. Managing suppliers effectively requires organization, communication, negotiation, forecasting, and relationship-building, all of which can be enhanced and automated using AI. This chapter teaches you how to structure your supplier operations so that AI becomes your assistant for negotiating better pricing, tracking catalog updates, monitoring stock availability, identifying new products, and communicating professionally at scale. The goal is to transform your supplier interactions into a reliable pipeline that feeds your business predictable inventory and long-term competitive advantage. The instructional foundation begins with understanding how AI can analyze supplier quality. Not all suppliers are equal, and many sellers waste time on suppliers who offer poor discounts, inconsistent availability, or catalogs filled with low-margin products. AI can evaluate supplier viability by reviewing historical pricing patterns, stock cycles, lead times, MAP compliance, product diversity, and responsiveness. You will learn to prompt AI to create supplier scorecards, which summarize each supplier's strengths and weaknesses in terms of profitability potential, communication quality, shipping reliability, and risk factors such as IP restrictions or erratic pricing. These scorecards allow you to prioritize high-value suppliers and reduce time spent on low-quality ones.

The next major instructional component involves training AI to manage supplier catalogs dynamically. Suppliers frequently update their price lists, run promotions, clear out seasonal stock, or add new items. Instead of manually reviewing each update, AI can scan new catalogs, identify newly added SKUs, highlight price changes, detect temporary markdowns, and cross-reference changes with your replenishment pipeline. AI can alert you when a profitable replenishable item has dropped in price, when a new item aligns with your sourcing criteria, or when a product you previously passed on now meets your margin requirements. This automation ensures you never miss valuable opportunities and helps you stay ahead of other sellers who evaluate catalogs manually.

Another instructional focus is automating supplier communication using AI. Many sellers struggle with writing professional emails, requesting price lists, negotiating discounts, or asking for better shipping terms. AI can generate polished, persuasive messages tailored to each supplier's tone and relationship history. It can help you draft negotiation scripts that explain why you need better pricing, how you plan to scale orders, or why your business is a valuable partner. You will learn how to empower AI to create follow-up sequences that maintain consistent communication with suppliers—ensuring that you remain top-of-mind when new deals or closeout opportunities arise. This system turns communication into a predictable part of your workflow instead of something you handle reactively.

The chapter continues by teaching you how AI can serve as a negotiation assistant. Supplier negotiations require strategy, timing, and data. AI can analyze your purchasing volume, compare prices across multiple suppliers, evaluate profit margins, and generate negotiation proposals that maximize your leverage. It can simulate negotiation responses, prepare counter-offers, and provide scripts that help you secure better cost prices, free shipping, or bulk discounts. AI can also detect inconsistencies in supplier quotes, ensuring that you catch hidden fees or pricing mistakes before committing. By leveraging AI in your negotiation process, you gain confidence and clarity that most sellers never experience.

Another important instructional component is using AI to track supplier inventory levels and stock cycles. Suppliers often run out of popular products or restock items on predictable schedules. AI can process supplier updates, emails, PDFs, and website notifications automatically, identifying which items are back in stock, which are running low, and which are being discontinued. You can train AI to notify you when high-demand items return or when limited quantities present an urgent buying window. This prevents missed opportunities and allows you to secure inventory before other sellers even realize it's available.

AI also plays a vital role in supplier compliance and risk management. Some brands enforce strict MAP policies, file IP complaints, or limit authorized seller lists. AI can analyze supplier terms, monitor brand behavior across Amazon, and identify suppliers who may present legal or account health risks. It can scan contracts for restrictive clauses, flag brands known for aggressive enforcement, and evaluate whether a supplier is an authorized distributor. This helps you avoid high-risk partnerships that could threaten your Amazon account or profitability. The final instructional element in this chapter is building a centralized AI-assisted supplier dashboard. This dashboard consolidates supplier scorecards, communication logs, order history, negotiation notes, catalog updates, AI profitability reports, and replenishment recommendations. Instead of managing suppliers through scattered emails and spreadsheets, you gain a structured system that provides visibility into your entire network. Over time, this dashboard becomes a strategic advantage—allowing you to track which suppliers deserve more of your business, which products should be scaled, and where new opportunities may arise. By integrating AI into supplier management, you elevate your business from reactive sourcing to proactive partnership-building, which is the key to long-term success in Amazon wholesale and arbitrage.

Daniel Noticed an Alert

Daniel always believed that suppliers controlled his destiny. If a supplier responded quickly, he felt hopeful. If a supplier ignored him, he felt defeated. If a supplier sent a good catalog, he felt like he was winning. But if they sent a list full of garbage, he felt like the week was already lost. For years, it felt like his business rose and fell on the whims of suppliers he barely knew. But as he sat at his desk staring at his new AI-powered supplier dashboard, he realized something profound. For the first time in his career, he wasn't at the mercy of suppliers—he was in control of the entire system.

One morning, he opened an email from a supplier he had worked with inconsistently for years. They had sent a new 200-item catalog. Normally, this would have required hours of tedious analysis. But Daniel uploaded it into his AI system and watched as the dashboard transformed the overwhelming list into a clean breakdown of opportunities: new profitable SKUs, existing replens with price drops, items with improved margins due to decreased shipping costs, and several products that looked unprofitable on the surface but revealed hidden potential after AI calculated multi-scenario profitability. He was stunned. It felt as if someone had lifted a weight off his shoulders—a weight he didn't realize he had been carrying for so long.

Later that afternoon, Daniel needed to request better pricing on a product that had recently become one of his best-sellers. In the past, negotiating with suppliers made him anxious. He always felt unsure of what to say or how to justify his requests. But now, he simply asked the AI to craft a negotiation message based on his order volume, past purchases, and future potential. The resulting email was persuasive, professional, and confident. Daniel sent it and expected to wait days for a reply. Instead, the supplier responded within an hour, offering him a bulk discount he had never received before. Daniel stared at the message, amazed. He hadn't realized how much more effectively he could communicate when AI gave him the right words.

A few days later, a different supplier sent him a price list with items marked as "limited stock." Daniel uploaded it into his system. The AI instantly flagged several risks: inconsistent past pricing, temporary profit spikes caused by stockouts, and high volatility in seller count. But it also identified one hidden gem—a product with stable margins, predictable demand, and strong evidence of future growth. Daniel felt a spark of excitement. He reached out to the supplier immediately, armed with an AI-generated message that expressed urgency and professionalism. Within minutes, he secured the remaining units before other sellers even looked at the list.

One evening, while reviewing his supplier dashboard, Daniel noticed an alert. AI detected that a product he had previously dismissed had reentered stock at a significantly lower cost. This time, the AI evaluated the new price and flagged it as a strong buy. Daniel verified the details manually, smiled, and placed an order. He would have missed this opportunity without AI. Instead, he was the first seller back in the game—giving him a temporary advantage in a listing that still had healthy demand.

Another breakthrough came unexpectedly. A supplier sent Daniel a contract to sign before granting him access to exclusive catalogs. In the past, Daniel had skimmed documents like this, hoping nothing important was hidden inside. But now, he uploaded it to the AI, which scanned it line by line. It flagged a restrictive clause that could have limited his resale rights. With AI's help, Daniel drafted a respectful request to amend the clause. To his surprise, the supplier agreed. He realized that without AI, he might have signed a contract that constrained his growth for years.

As the weeks went on, Daniel noticed how calm he felt when dealing with suppliers. He no longer worried about missing opportunities, forgetting follow-ups, or misinterpreting catalog changes. He no longer felt intimidated by negotiations or unsure when evaluating contracts. His AI system had become his advisor, his assistant, and his second brain—helping him see everything clearly, confidently, and strategically.

One night, as he reviewed his supplier dashboard before closing his laptop, Daniel felt a deep sense of gratitude. What once felt chaotic now felt organized. What once felt uncertain now felt predictable. And what once felt overwhelming now felt like a game he finally knew how to win. Suppliers were no longer gatekeepers. They were now partners in a system he had built with precision and intelligence.

Daniel smiled, knowing he had just crossed another threshold in his journey. He wasn't just sourcing products anymore. He was building relationships, negotiating strategically, forecasting intelligently, and managing suppliers with a level of mastery he never thought possible. And tomorrow, with AI by his side, he would do it even better.

Chapter 8

Competitor Monitoring & Price Forecasting With AI: Anticipating Market Moves Before They Happen

Chapter 8 introduces one of the most powerful and often misunderstood capabilities of AI in the Amazon wholesale and arbitrage ecosystem: competitor monitoring and AI-powered price forecasting. While many sellers obsess over sourcing and profitability analysis, the sellers who achieve long-term stability and growth are those who understand the dynamics of competition and pricing on Amazon. The marketplace is constantly shifting. Sellers enter and exit listings, prices rise and fall, Amazon restocks, brand owners adjust strategies, and seasonal cycles create predictable and unpredictable changes. The goal of this chapter is to teach you how to leverage AI to monitor these movements continuously and use advanced prediction models to anticipate market changes before they happen. With this advantage, your decisions become proactive rather than reactive, resulting in better margins, smarter buy quantities, and fewer costly mistakes.

The instructional foundation begins with competitor behavior analysis. AI can examine seller patterns in ways the human mind cannot replicate. It can track historical seller count, observe buy box rotation trends, identify sellers who frequently appear in your categories, and detect aggressive repricers that may push prices downward. You will learn how to create AI prompts that analyze seller types—whether they are casual arbitrage sellers, professional wholesalers, or Amazon itself. AI can determine whether a new seller joining the listing is likely to tank prices or simply coexist with stable pricing. This insight allows you to avoid listings where volatility is tied to inexperienced sellers repeatedly undercutting the market.

Another key instructional concept involves monitoring the buy box competition using AI. The buy box is the heartbeat of every listing, dictating who gets the sale and at what price. AI can analyze buy box changes at scale, track how often Amazon holds the buy box, identify when buy box price increases or decreases correlate with seller entry or exit, and calculate the probability that you can win the buy box with your fulfillment method. You will learn how to use AI to detect patterns like predictable price dips during specific times of day, temporary undercutting by inexperienced sellers, or buy box suppression caused by listing errors. By monitoring these patterns, you can prepare more accurate profitability projections.

The chapter then advances into AI-powered price forecasting. Price forecasting involves using historical data, category trends, seasonal cycles, competitor behavior, and Amazon's stocking fluctuations to predict future prices. AI can analyze long-term pricing graphs, identify price floors and ceilings, and pinpoint the most likely price ranges over the next 30, 60, or 90 days. You will learn how to prompt AI to detect when a price drop is temporary due to a stockout, when a price spike is artificial due to limited sellers, and when long-term decline indicates a collapsing listing. With this forecasting ability, you can make smarter purchasing decisions, choosing products that will remain profitable instead of those that only look profitable at the moment.

Another important instructional focus is AI-driven sales velocity projection. AI can interpret subtle shifts in demand by monitoring changes in rank, review growth, customer question activity, and competitor inventory levels. When certain sellers run out of stock, demand shifts toward the remaining sellers, temporarily increasing their velocity and margins. AI can predict these moments and notify you when an opportunity emerges. Additionally, AI can forecast whether sales velocity will remain strong or weaken due to category trends, seasonal fluctuations, or decreasing customer interest. This gives you a clear understanding of how quickly your inventory will turn and when it is safe to scale. A significant part of this chapter focuses on AI-based repricer analysis. While you may not use a repricer yourself, your competitors often do. AI can detect repricing strategies and categorize competitor repricers as aggressive, passive, oscillating, or rule-based. This helps you avoid listings where repricers create destructive price wars. AI can analyze how quickly prices fall after new sellers enter, how low prices typically drop, and how long it takes for prices to recover. This insight is critical for determining whether a listing is truly healthy or vulnerable to recurring margin erosion.

Next, you learn how to combine competitor monitoring and price forecasting with your sourcing system. AI can automatically evaluate your current buys and warn you if a previously stable listing is showing early signs of competition spikes or price instability. It can also analyze supplier catalogs in real time and determine whether new opportunities align with current market conditions. The integration of these systems allows you to build a sourcing pipeline that evolves with the marketplace rather than becoming obsolete when conditions change.

The final instructional takeaway of this chapter is creating AI-driven alerts that notify you when specific competitive or pricing conditions occur. You can set alerts for sudden price drops, unusual seller entries, Amazon restock events, suppressed buy boxes, and rapid shifts in rank. These alerts give you the ability to act instantly and strategically—either pausing purchases, accelerating reorders, adjusting pricing strategy, or liquidating slow-moving inventory. When used correctly, AI becomes your watchtower, monitoring your listings continuously and protecting your margins with insights that human sellers could never gather fast enough. By mastering competitor monitoring and price forecasting, you obtain one of the most valuable advantages in the Amazon marketplace: foresight.

The AI Displayed a Breakdown

Daniel had always known that competition on Amazon was fierce, but the deeper he went into wholesale and arbitrage, the more he realized that success wasn't about finding products—it was about understanding people. Sellers behaved in patterns: some patient, some reckless, some desperate, some disciplined, some unpredictable enough to destroy the profitability of an entire listing. In his early days, Daniel felt like he was reacting to chaos. When prices dropped, he panicked. When new sellers joined a listing, he felt anxious. When demand dropped unexpectedly, he blamed bad luck. But tonight, as he sat in his office watching his AI competitor monitoring dashboard update in real time, he realized that luck had nothing to do with it. There were patterns everywhere. He had simply never been able to see them before.

The AI displayed a breakdown of one of his top-performing products. Daniel noticed that a new seller had entered the listing. Normally, this would make him uneasy. But the AI had analyzed the seller's past behavior. It revealed that this seller typically listed only a handful of units, priced conservatively, and rarely triggered price wars. Daniel felt an unexpected sense of calm. The AI wasn't just showing him data—it was showing him personality. It was showing him the rhythm of the marketplace, the push and pull of seller decisions, the hidden signals beneath the surface.

Later that afternoon, Daniel received a notification. The AI detected a sudden buy box drop on one of his beauty products. A year ago, he would have assumed the listing was tanking. But now, AI explained that the dip was caused by a temporary stockout from two major competitors and that the price was expected to rebound within a week. Daniel checked the forecast graph. The prediction made sense. Instead of panicking or lowering his own price, he held firm. Three days later, the buy box returned to its original level, and Daniel sold his inventory at full margin. Without AI, he would have caved under pressure and lost profit. With AI, he stayed steady.

One evening, Daniel uploaded a new supplier catalog and watched AI cross-reference each product with competitive data. One item—a home improvement tool—stood out. The margins looked great, but the AI flagged a deeper risk. It showed that every time new sellers entered the listing, prices dropped sharply within 48 hours. The AI displayed a historical pattern of repricer-driven price wars. Daniel stared at the graph. It looked like a battlefield—sharp drops, chaotic spikes, unpredictable recoveries. He closed the listing instantly, grateful that the AI had spared him from a costly trap he would have walked into months earlier.

A few days later, Daniel experienced the opposite scenario. Another product—a kitchen accessory—had a small profit margin at first glance. He almost dismissed it. But the AI revealed something unexpected. The seller count had been declining steadily for weeks. Amazon had gone out of stock. The buy box price had risen quietly and consistently. Competitors were selling out one by one. And the AI forecasted a strong upward price trend for the next 30 days. Daniel felt a surge of excitement. This was more than an opportunity—it was timing. Perfect timing. He placed an order immediately. When the units arrived and he sent them in, the listing exploded. The price climbed exactly as predicted, and Daniel captured the best margins of the season.

As weeks passed, Daniel found himself forming an almost intuitive bond with his AI system. He could sense when competition was shifting. He could anticipate price drops before they happened. He could recognize which sellers posed real threats and which were harmless. AI wasn't removing uncertainty—it was illuminating it. For the first time, Daniel didn't feel like he was playing defense. He was playing offense.

One night, as he looked over his price forecasting dashboard, Daniel felt something he hadn't felt in years: control. Real control. The marketplace no longer felt like a storm he had to survive. It felt like a map he could read. Every movement made sense. Every pattern told a story. Every seller's behavior, every price shift, every rank fluctuation—AI translated it all into clarity.

Daniel leaned back in his chair, feeling a sense of mastery settling over him. He finally understood the real power of AI. It wasn't just finding products or calculating profits. It was giving him eyes—eyes that could see the future. And with that clarity, Daniel knew he was no longer just participating in the Amazon marketplace. He was learning how to shape it.

Chapter 9

Financial Intelligence, Cash Flow & Profit Forecasting: Turning Amazon Data Into Predictable Business Performance

Chapter 9 focuses on a powerful, revenue-transforming capability of AI: automating your financial tracking, forecasting, and business intelligence systems so your Amazon wholesale and arbitrage operation becomes predictable, stable, scalable, and strategically guided by data rather than guesswork. Many sellers struggle not because they lack profitable products, but because they lack clarity. They do not know their true profit after all costs. They do not know how much cash is tied up in inventory. They cannot accurately predict when their next payout will be large or small. They do not know which SKUs carry their business and which quietly drain their capital. This lack of visibility creates anxiety, inconsistent decision-making, and unnecessary risk. In this chapter, you will learn how to use AI to build a complete financial intelligence system that automatically analyzes your sales, expenses, forecasts, and SKU-level performance with precision that manual spreadsheets could never achieve. The instructional foundation begins by teaching you how to use AI to interpret your Amazon financial data. Amazon's Seller Central reports are notoriously confusing, with fees scattered across multiple categories and payout summaries that hide important information. AI can process settlement reports, SKU-level fee breakdowns, FBA shipment costs, restock fees, removal fees, storage costs, reimbursements, and even refund deductions. By feeding these reports into AI, you can receive a clear, organized, and categorized summary of your financial activity. This eliminates the guesswork and gives you the ability to see, in real time, the financial health of your business. You will learn how to prompt AI to create expense summaries, trend reports, fee analyses, and profit tracking dashboards.

The next instructional component teaches you how AI can create SKU-level performance intelligence. Not all products contribute equally to your business. Some SKUs generate massive profit with little maintenance. Others produce weak margins or carry hidden costs like high return rates or oversized FBA fees. AI can evaluate each SKU's contribution to revenue, total profit, sell-through consistency, volatility, and capital efficiency. You will learn how to use AI to rank SKUs by profitability, identify underperforming products, and highlight which SKUs deserve scaling. This transforms your decision-making. Instead of trying to scale products randomly, you will scale those with the strongest financial and behavioral patterns. Instead of keeping products that merely "sell," you will focus on those that actually grow your business sustainably.

Another critical instructional area is cash flow forecasting. Amazon payouts can be unpredictable, especially when you're growing rapidly or buying inventory in large batches. AI can analyze past payout cycles, sales velocity patterns, upcoming inventory arrivals, and cost structures to predict future payouts. It can determine whether your next payout will be larger or smaller, how much capital you can safely reinvest, and when you should expect liquidity constraints. You will learn how to build prompts that ask AI to calculate your projected cash flow for the next 2, 4, 8, or 12 weeks. This foresight allows you to avoid overinvesting, missing replenishment opportunities, or creating capital bottlenecks that slow your growth.

Another powerful instructional component is building an AI profit forecasting model. Profit forecasting involves projecting not just revenue but true net profit after all expenses. AI can run multi-scenario forecasts simulating different conditions such as minor price drops, unexpected competition, increased storage fees, or seasonal slowdowns. By teaching AI to simulate these situations, you gain the ability to make purchasing decisions with a deeper understanding of potential outcomes. You will no longer rely on hope or instinct. Instead, you will have a data-driven predictive model guiding your actions. The chapter also introduces AI-driven expense classification. Many sellers fail to track their expenses accurately because they are overwhelmed by the number of small, recurring charges that accumulate—software subscriptions, prep center fees, packing materials, VA costs, shipping supplies, PPC spend, storage fees, and more. AI can automatically categorize your expenses, calculate monthly cost patterns, and identify areas where you can reduce waste. This gives you clarity and control over your operational expenses and helps you maintain strong profit margins even as your business scales.

Next, you will learn how AI can consolidate all of this intelligence into a business dashboard. This dashboard becomes the heartbeat of your operation. It provides real-time updates on profit, revenue, sales velocity, inventory value, upcoming payouts, SKU performance, and financial projections. AI can refresh this dashboard continuously, ensuring you always know the pulse of your business without manually pulling reports or calculating numbers. Over time, your dashboard becomes your command center, allowing you to run your business with precision.

The final instructional takeaway of this chapter is creating AI alerts for financial risks and opportunities. AI can notify you when storage fees spike, when a SKU's profitability declines, when your cash flow is trending downward, or when your expenses exceed your budget. It can also alert you to positive opportunities such as unexpected profitability spikes, faster-than-expected sales velocity, or low-risk scaling opportunities. With this system, you operate with complete financial visibility and confidence. You no longer guess. You know. And when you know, you make decisions that lead to long-term success rather than short-term survival.

The Ai Wasn't Just Analyzing Data—It Was Protecting Him

Daniel had always thought he was doing fine financially—at least until tax season arrived each year and exposed all the gaps he didn't want to admit were there. Some months felt amazing, full of high payouts and steady sales, while others felt confusing and frustrating, with less money in his bank account than he expected. He often wondered where the profit went. He wondered why certain SKUs seemed great but never actually increased his income. And he wondered how other sellers seemed so calm and confident when he always felt like he was navigating in the dark. But everything changed the day he built his AI financial dashboard.

It began one quiet morning. Daniel downloaded his latest settlement report and fed it into the AI. He expected the usual summary: payouts, fees, and basic numbers. But instead, the AI generated a detailed breakdown—every fee category, every SKU-level deduction, every hidden cost he had overlooked for years. It grouped his expenses, highlighted inefficiencies, calculated true net profit, and displayed everything in an organized format he could understand instantly. Daniel stared at the screen, stunned. For the first time in his entire Amazon career, the numbers made sense.

Later that afternoon, the AI analyzed his SKU-level performance. Daniel expected his top-selling SKUs to also be his most profitable. But the AI revealed a different story. One SKU that generated high revenue turned out to be draining his profit due to steep FBA fees and high return rates. Another SKU he barely thought about was producing some of his highest margins. Daniel felt a mix of shock and clarity wash over him. He realized he had been making decisions based on impressions rather than data. And in that moment, he felt a powerful shift inside him. He wasn't just seeing numbers—he was seeing truth.

A few days later, Daniel experienced the first major breakthrough. The AI generated a cash flow projection and warned him that his upcoming payout would be lower because he had recently placed a large wholesale order. Without this insight, Daniel might have overextended his purchases or missed opportunities by tying up too much capital. But now, he saw exactly how his cash flow would move over the next four weeks. He could plan his purchases intelligently. He could anticipate his liquidity. He could finally breathe without anxiety hanging over his decisions. It was as if someone had turned on the lights in a room he had been navigating blindly for years.

One evening, Daniel ran a profit simulation for a new product he was considering. The AI calculated multiple pricing scenarios and revealed that although the current buy box price looked healthy, even a small drop in price would destroy profitability. It showed how competition patterns could impact margin stability and why the product posed more risk than reward. A year ago, Daniel would have bought deep into this product and learned the lesson the hard way. But now, he felt empowered. The AI wasn't just analyzing data—it was protecting him from his own optimism.

A few weeks later, the AI dashboard delivered an unexpected insight. One of Daniel's smaller SKUs, one he barely noticed, was quietly generating consistent profit every single week. The AI recommended scaling it. Daniel placed a larger order, uploaded the new batch, and watched as the sales flowed in effortlessly. It felt like discovering treasure hidden in plain sight. And it made him realize something profound: without AI, he had been blind to the true drivers of his business.

One night, while reviewing his updated dashboard, Daniel saw his entire operation displayed with clarity he never thought possible—profit trends, payout forecasts, SKU rankings, upcoming inventory needs, and cash flow projections. It felt like looking at the inside of his business's brain. Everything connected. Everything made sense. For the first time, he didn't feel like a seller chasing opportunities. He felt like a business owner guiding a machine that he built, a machine that finally worked with precision.

As he closed his laptop, Daniel smiled to himself. He had entered the Amazon world years ago hoping to earn extra income. But now, he understood what it meant to run a real operation. AI had given him sight, strategy, and control. And Chapter 9 of his journey was not just about tracking numbers—it was about transforming his business into something intelligent, stable, and scalable. His future no longer felt uncertain. It felt designed.

Chapter 10

Building a Fully Automated AI Amazon Operation: Integrating Sourcing, Inventory, Finance, and Strategy Into One System

Chapter 10 focuses on one of the most transformative capabilities available to modern Amazon sellers: building fully integrated AI workflows that automate the majority of your business operations from sourcing to fulfillment to financial management. Up to this point, each chapter has taught you how AI can assist with individual functions—catalog analysis, profitability forecasting, competitor monitoring, inventory management, and supplier relations. Now, this chapter shows you how to connect all those systems into a unified, automated machine that works continuously with minimal human intervention. The goal of this chapter is simple but powerful: to help you build an AI-driven wholesale and arbitrage business that runs smoother, faster, and more accurately than any system you could manage manually.

The instructional foundation begins by teaching you how to integrate your sourcing pipeline with your profitability engine. Instead of treating sourcing as a separate task, AI can automatically funnel new supplier catalogs, retail clearance lists, online deals, or emailed spreadsheets into your profitability model. This integration allows AI to evaluate every new opportunity instantly and categorize it according to your sourcing criteria, risk thresholds, and inventory needs. You will learn how to structure prompts that instruct AI to automatically analyze incoming data, eliminate unqualified products, and add promising opportunities directly to your sourcing shortlist. This reduces manual workload dramatically and ensures that every sourcing decision is grounded in real-time financial insights.

The next instructional component teaches you how to connect your competitor analysis system to your replenishment workflow. AI can monitor seller count, pricing movements, Amazon restock behavior, and category volatility, then automatically adjust your replenishment recommendations based on this data. For example, if competition begins rising on a product, AI may reduce your reorder quantity or flag the SKU as requiring closer monitoring. If competition decreases or price stability improves, AI may recommend scaling deeper. Instead of manually interpreting market signals, you gain a self-adjusting inventory system that continuously adapts to marketplace changes. This prevents overbuying, underbuying, and costly misjudgments. Another major instructional focus is automating communication and supplier workflow management. You will learn how AI can read emails from suppliers, extract relevant data, update your supplier dashboards, identify new catalogs, respond with pre-written negotiation templates, and flag urgent messages requiring human review. AI can also generate reorder emails, request updated price lists, follow up on quotes, and send polite reminders when communication lags. When integrated correctly, AI becomes your 24/7 administrative assistant, ensuring no opportunity is missed and no communication thread goes unmanaged. This frees you to focus on creativity, strategy, and expansion rather than admin work.

The chapter then explores integrating AI financial analysis with sourcing and inventory management. Instead of evaluating profit metrics manually, the AI can run full financial simulations automatically every time a new opportunity is detected. It can determine whether a product fits your budget, whether your cash flow allows for scaling, and whether the item aligns with your long-term profitability goals. AI can forecast your ability to replenish the product sustainably and warn you if buying the product would create a liquidity bottleneck. This ensures that your decisions are cohesive across all operating areas rather than isolated, inconsistent judgments.

You will also learn how to create AI systems that identify growth opportunities automatically. AI can detect product lines where you have strong momentum, categories where you consistently outperform competitors, and supplier relationships that offer untapped potential. It can recommend expanding into adjacent SKUs, bundling items into new listings, or exploring additional suppliers for categories where you are already profitable. Instead of forcing yourself to find growth opportunities blindly, AI reveals them through data intelligence. This transforms scaling from guesswork into a strategic, guided process.

Another powerful instructional concept in this chapter is building AI-driven risk control systems. AI can monitor historical volatility, Amazon involvement, price crashes, seasonal fluctuations, and competitor behavior across your entire catalog. When risk conditions exceed your preset thresholds, AI can trigger alerts, recommend liquidation strategies, or remove SKUs from your replenishment pipeline. This protects your capital and ensures your business remains focused on stable, long-term profit rather than chasing unstable opportunities.

The final instructional takeaway of this chapter is understanding how to orchestrate all these components into a single AI-driven operational ecosystem. When properly integrated, your AI will continuously scan for deals, evaluate their profitability, monitor competitor activity, track finances, manage communication, forecast demand, and optimize inventory levels. You are no longer running individual tasks—you are overseeing a machine. This automated system does not rely on mood, fatigue, or guesswork. It performs with consistent accuracy and speed, providing you with a business that runs more predictably and with less stress. By mastering full AI workflow integration, you position yourself for long-term success, scalability, and sustainability in one of the most competitive marketplaces in the world.

Something Remarkable Had Happened

Daniel had never felt more in control of his business than he did the night he watched all his AI systems begin to work together—truly work together—for the first time. He sat back, sipping a cup of coffee as the screens in front of him lit up with synchronized data. His sourcing tool was scanning a newly uploaded supplier catalog automatically. His profitability engine evaluated each item instantly. His competitor dashboard monitored alerts. His financial AI updated projections. And his replenishment system was already calculating which SKUs would need new orders next week. For the first time, Daniel wasn't using a collection of tools. He was operating a machine—an interconnected, intelligent system that felt alive.

Earlier that day, something remarkable had happened. A supplier emailed him a new price list without warning. Normally, Daniel would have skimmed it quickly, saved it for later, or forgotten about it until the weekend. But his AI email system detected the attachment, extracted the catalog, and processed it automatically. By the time Daniel checked his dashboard, the AI had already analyzed every item, flagged new opportunities, and added three potential winners to his shortlist. It had even drafted a message to the supplier requesting volume pricing on one of the promising SKUs. Daniel didn't have to think. He only needed to click send. The speed, efficiency, and precision felt unreal.

Later in the afternoon, another AI system triggered an alert. A competitor who had been aggressively undercutting one of Daniel's best sellers suddenly sold out. The buy box price jumped. Daniel's replenishment engine recalculated expected profits and recommended increasing his next order quantity. Meanwhile, his financial AI confirmed that cash flow supported the purchase. His entire operation reacted instantly in perfect synchronization. Daniel felt a thrill rush through him. This wasn't selling anymore. This was strategy in motion. This was a business executing itself.

One moment stuck with him more than any other. Daniel had been considering a new product all week. It had strong margins, but something about it didn't sit right in his gut. In the past, he would have debated the decision endlessly. But now, with AI integration, the answer found him. His competitor monitoring system flagged the listing as unstable due to recurring price wars triggered by new sellers. His financial engine revealed that even small price drops would break profitability. His replenishment system indicated the product wouldn't fit well into his long-term inventory strategy. Three separate systems—all independent, all intelligent—delivered the same conclusion. Without hesitation, Daniel walked away from the deal. There was no fear, no regret, no uncertainty. Only clarity.

That evening, something unexpected happened. Daniel received a congratulatory email from one of his suppliers thanking him for his consistent communication, professionalism, and timely responses. Daniel laughed. It wasn't him. It was his AI communication system, maintaining contact, following up, requesting updates, and nurturing the relationship quietly in the background. For years, Daniel struggled to keep track of conversations, missed messages, or forgot to respond in the chaos of daily operations. Now, relationships flourished effortlessly. Suppliers saw him as reliable, professional, and engaged. It felt like having an administrative assistant who never forgot anything, never got tired, and never made mistakes.

As the night grew quieter, Daniel took a moment to appreciate what he had built. He remembered the anxiety he used to feel—running out of stock unexpectedly, missing great deals because he was overwhelmed, buying into bad listings because he didn't have enough data, losing money due to unpredictable competition, and never really knowing how much profit he was making. All of that felt distant now. He looked at his interconnected AI systems humming steadily, each one feeding into the next like gears in a perfectly engineered machine.

He realized something profound about his journey. AI hadn't replaced him. It had amplified him. It had sharpened his instincts, strengthened his decisions, eliminated his weaknesses, and expanded his capabilities. It gave him something he had never truly felt in his business before: peace. Peace because everything made sense. Peace because every decision was grounded in intelligence. Peace because he wasn't alone in the complexity anymore. He had built a system that saw everything, predicted everything, and connected everything.

Daniel closed his laptop, leaned back in his chair, and smiled. His business wasn't just growing. It was evolving—becoming smarter, faster, and more powerful than he ever imagined. And for the first time, he felt ready for whatever the marketplace would bring next. He wasn't reacting to the future. He was preparing for it. He was designing it. And tomorrow, with AI guiding every part of his operation, he would build something even greater.

Final Thoughts

The journey through this book has revealed a truth that many Amazon sellers never discover: success is not determined by how hard you work, how long you stare at spreadsheets, or how quickly you scan shelves. Success is determined by how intelligently you operate, how effectively you use information, and how consistently your systems perform in your place. The rise of AI has transformed the Amazon wholesale and arbitrage world from a chaotic, unpredictable arena into a structured environment where data, forecasting, automation, and strategy guide every decision. As you reach the end of this book, the most important realization is that you now possess the ability to build a business that is not only profitable, but sustainable—one that adapts, grows, and evolves with the marketplace.

This epilogue invites you to reflect on how far you have come. Perhaps when you started your Amazon journey, you felt overwhelmed by the sheer amount of work involved: sourcing products manually, evaluating listings one by one, guessing margins, struggling with supplier communication, and reacting to unpredictable price changes. You may have felt anxious each time you placed an order, unsure whether your investment would pay off. You may have looked at competitors who seemed effortlessly successful and wondered what secrets they knew that you didn't. Now, those days feel distant. Through the lessons in this book, you have learned to transform uncertainty into clarity and chaos into precision.

You now understand that AI is not merely a tool—it is an operating system for your business. It analyzes supplier catalogs faster than any human. It forecasts profitability with more accuracy than any instinct. It monitors competitors tirelessly, without emotion, fatigue, or bias. It creates financial transparency that replaces confusion with certainty. It becomes your negotiator, your analyst, your strategist, your researcher, your inventory manager, and your silent partner. With AI, you no longer guess—you know. You no longer hope—you plan. You no longer react—you anticipate. And with this evolution, your business enters a new chapter defined not by luck but by design.

As you integrate the systems you've built—sourcing automation, profitability engines, replenishment forecasting, competitor analysis, supplier management, and financial intelligence—you are constructing something rare: an Amazon business capable of scaling without sacrificing your time, energy, or peace of mind. You are no longer building a job. You are building a machine. The compounding effects of these systems will continue to strengthen your operation each month, revealing opportunities you once overlooked and protecting you from risks that once held you back. The more you trust your data-driven foundation, the more growth becomes natural, predictable, and repeatable.

Yet the true transformation is not merely operational. It is internal. You now see the market differently. Patterns that once felt random now feel predictable. Competition that once intimidated you now feels manageable. Financial numbers that once confused you now feel like a language you can read fluently. You have become someone who *understands* the Amazon ecosystem on a deeper level—a strategist rather than a participant, a builder rather than a reactor. AI didn't just improve your workflow. It expanded your perspective, sharpened your judgment, and elevated the way you think about business.

As you move forward, new challenges will arise. The marketplace will evolve. New competitors will emerge. Trends will shift, and unexpected changes will appear. But with the systems you have developed, you are no longer vulnerable to these changes. Instead, you are prepared for them. You have built a resilient foundation capable of adapting automatically, guided by data rather than emotion. Every challenge becomes an opportunity for refinement. Every shift becomes a chance to strengthen your competitive advantage. You no longer fear the future—you shape it. This book is not the conclusion of your journey. It is the beginning of a new phase—one where your business has structure, intelligence, automation, and power. A phase where you operate with clarity, confidence, and control. A phase where your success is no longer dependent on grinding through tasks but on orchestrating systems. As you apply what you've learned, your business will grow not only in revenue but in stability, precision, and predictability. And that is the true purpose of AI in wholesale and arbitrage: to give you freedom—the freedom to scale, to innovate, to strategize, and ultimately, to build a business that supports the life you want.

Take a moment to acknowledge the transformation. You began with questions, concerns, and uncertainties. You now carry tools, frameworks, and clarity. The path ahead is wide open, and you have everything you need to walk it with skill and confidence. Let your systems work for you. Let AI amplify your strengths. And let this book be the foundation of a smarter, stronger, and more scalable Amazon business. The next chapter belongs to you—and with AI by your side, it will be extraordinary.

www.ingramcontent.com/pod-product-compliance
Lightning Source LLC
LaVergne TN
LVHW022010200926
848481LV00007B/2320
* 9 7 9 8 2 9 5 4 8 7 9 7 2 *